304.2

Morris, N.

Living on islands

WHERE PEOPLE LIVE

Living on Islands

Neil Morris

W

FRANKLIN WATTS
LONDON•SYDNEY

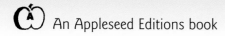 An Appleseed Editions book

First published in 2004 by Franklin Watts
96 Leonard Street, London, EC2A 4XD

Franklin Watts Australia
45–51 Huntley Street, Alexandria, NSW 2015

Created by Appleseed Editions Ltd,
Well House, Friars Hill, Guestling, East Sussex, TN35 4ET

Designed by Helen James

ISBN 0 7496 5836 3

A CIP catalogue for this book is available from the British Library.

Photographs by Corbis (Tony Arruza, Richard Cummins, Bennett Dean; Eye Ubiquitous, Rick Doyle, Robert Essel NYC, Macduff Everton, Jack Fields, Stephen Frink, Raymond Gehman, GIRAUD PHILIPPE/CORBIS SYGMA, Farrell Grehan, Peter Guttman, HARUYOSHI YAMAGUCHI/CORBIS SYGMA, Wolfgang Kaehler, Bob Krist, Daniel Lainé, Christophe Loviny, Buddy Mays, Mike McQueen, Gail Mooney, Peter Philipp; Viennaslide Photoagency, Roger Ressmeyer, Hans Georg Roth, Kevin Schafer, Paul A. Souders, Tim Thompson, Denis Anthony Valentine, Stuart Westmorland, Nik Wheeler, Peter M. Wilson, Adam Woolfitt)

Printed in the USA

Contents

Introduction

An island is a piece of land that is surrounded by water. The biggest island in the world is Greenland, which is actually part of another country (Denmark) that lies thousands of miles away. Australia and Antarctica are also surrounded by water, but they are so big that they are called continents. Some islands, such as Madagascar and Iceland, are separate countries in themselves. Others, such as the Philippines, are grouped together to form a **nation**. The Philippines is made up of more than 7,000 islands, though many are very small, and only about 900 of them are inhabited. Many people on the smaller islands are dependent on fishing, while rice and other crops are grown on **terraces** cut into the slopes of the larger, hilly islands.

▲ *Fishing in the Philippines. Fishing is an important industry on many of the world's islands.*

New Guinea

New Guinea lies in the Pacific Ocean, just south of the **equator**. It is the second largest island in the world (Greenland is the largest), and its people are divided into two nations. The western half, called Irian Jaya, belongs to Indonesia, and has many different **tribal groups** with their own

Some groups in Papua New Guinea continue to hold their traditional ceremonies.

languages and traditions. The eastern half, called Papua New Guinea, has a larger population – more than four million. The whole island is mountainous and covered in forests, but in recent times, more and more of the inland peoples have moved to towns and villages along the coast.

Land of fire and ice

The island of Iceland is icy, as its name suggests, but its glaciers lie next to steaming hot springs and fiery volcanoes, making it a truly dramatic island. Most Icelanders live near the coast, and many make their living from fishing. About half of all Icelanders live in the capital, Reykjavik. Their **ancestors**, who were mainly Vikings, created the world's first **parliament**. Called the 'Althing' and first held in 930, this parliament was a large meeting of the settlers who had sailed to Iceland from Norway. They later sailed on to other islands.

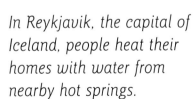

In Reykjavik, the capital of Iceland, people heat their homes with water from nearby hot springs.

Ancient Civilizations

Historians believe that modern humans first appeared a very long time ago in Africa. About 100,000 years ago, groups of them began making their way into Asia. These early people were hunter-gatherers. As they moved around, they hunted wild animals and gathered fruits, berries and roots for food. Many of them travelled along the coast because there they could catch fish. Once the people of later civilizations learned how to make and sail canoes, rafts and other boats, they were able to reach and discover islands that no one had visited before. Trading peoples, such as the ancient Phoenicians of the Mediterranean Sea, set up small villages and created **colonies** on islands.

▲ *The Phoenicians founded cities on the Mediterranean islands of Sicily, Sardinia and Corsica. These are the ruins at Nora, on the southern coast of Sardinia, which now belongs to Italy.*

Circle of Delos

The Cyclades are a group of more than 200 islands in the Aegean Sea. They got their name from the Greek word *kyklos*, meaning 'circle', because the ancient Greeks thought they formed a circle around the tiny island of Delos. According to legend, Delos was formed when the king of the ancient Greek gods, Zeus, anchored a rock to the seabed with columns of diamonds. The first people to settle the islands

These ancient houses were dug up on the island of Thera, in the Cyclades. They were preserved under layers of volcanic ash, allowing scientists to see how people lived on the island thousands of years ago.

came from Asia Minor (present-day Turkey), probably around 9,000 years ago. The ancient civilization of the Cyclades, called the Cycladic culture, began when the ancient islanders discovered how to make bronze (a metal made of a mixture of copper and tin) around 3000 BC.

Cyprus

The Mediterranean island of Cyprus lies to the east of the Cyclades. People have lived there for many thousands of years. In ancient times, the island was conquered by the Phoenicians, Assyrians, Egyptians, Persians, Macedonians and Romans. Cyprus has continued to change hands since then. First, the Venetians took control of it, then the British. It finally became an independent country in 1960, but there are still divisions between the Greek and Turkish people who live on the island today.

According to legend, the Greek goddess Aphrodite was born and came out of the sea on the coast of Cyprus. Her birthplace is known as the 'Rock of Aphrodite'.

Traditional Islanders

There are more than 20,000 islands in the world's largest ocean, the Pacific. Some are very small, and many of the people who live there are descended from those who first sailed to the islands from south-east Asia thousands of years ago. One large group of scattered islands is known as Polynesia, meaning 'many islands'. Many Polynesian seafarers (sailors) today still use the sailing methods of their ancestors. They steer large sailing canoes by the position of the sun and stars, studying the sea for patterns of waves and currents. They also look up at the sky to watch the movement of clouds and birds, and use maps made of sticks, pebbles and shells to pass on their knowledge.

▲ *Modern researchers have built replicas – copies, such as this one – of ancient Polynesian* **double-hulled** *sailing canoes.*

The Polynesian islanders' way of life is changing, as modern ways replace traditional methods. But they know that there is still a great deal to learn from those who first reached their islands.

People of the Long White Cloud

The Maori are a Polynesian people of New Zealand. They were the first inhabitants of that island country, which they call *Aotearoa* (meaning 'Land of the Long White Cloud').

Maori villagers traditionally met at a central courtyard, called a marae, which had a wooden meeting house beside it.

One legend says that the Maori arrived in seven canoes. Another says that an ancient hero created their country's North Island by fishing it up from the sea. The Maori probably sailed from other Polynesian islands about 1,000 years ago. At first they lived by fishing and by hunting large, flightless birds called moas. Today, some Maoris still uphold their traditional customs, such as worshipping the spirits of their dead ancestors.

Queen Charlotte Islands

The Queen Charlotte Islands lie more than 11,000 kilometres across the Pacific Ocean from New Zealand, off the coast of Canada. This group of about 150 islands is the traditional home of the Haida tribe of Native Americans. The Haida once lived near the shore in wooden houses made of long planks of cedar wood. They fished in the ocean from dugout canoes. These large boats, hollowed from tree trunks, were up to 20 metres long, and the Haida fishermen fished from them using hooks, nets and even **harpoons**. Today the islands form part of the Canadian province of British Columbia.

Haida **totem poles**, which featured carved animals from ancient tribal legends, were built into the front of plank houses.

Island Cities

In some parts of the world, islanders developed their small settlements into large towns. Some of these continued to grow into island cities. Two of the most famous are in North America. Manhattan Island forms one of the five **boroughs** of the continent's biggest city, New York. In 1626, the governor of a Dutch colony bought the island from local Algonquian Native Americans, who called it *Manahatta* ('Island of the Hills'). The Dutch renamed it New Amsterdam, and the original village grew into the city of New York. More than 480 kilometres further north lies the island of Montreal, in present-day Canada. Originally inhabited by the Iroquois, the island fell into French hands in 1642, when colonists built a fort and established a settlement there. Over many years, the settlement grew into the city of Montreal. Today, both these cities are joined to other islands and the mainland by bridges and tunnels.

Today, about two-thirds of the population of Montreal are French Canadians.

City between the Bridges

Stockholm, the capital of Sweden, is built on 14 islands in the Baltic Sea. The islands are connected by 50 bridges, and the old heart of the city is known as the 'City between the Bridges'. In the 1250s, Stockholm was founded as a fortress, surrounded by **stockades**, which later grew into an important trading centre. In 1523, the island city became the capital of Sweden. Today, many of the medieval streets of the city have been turned into pedestrian precincts full of antique shops and restaurants. Some of the modern city has spread to the nearby mainland.

Gateway to Asia

In 1534, a settlement was founded on an island in the Arabian Sea, just off the coast of India. The Sultan of Gujarat gave the island to the Portuguese, who called the settlement *Bom Bahia*, meaning 'good bay'. The growing city of 'Bombay' was British from 1661 until India gained independence in 1947. Today it is often known by its name in the Marathi language, Mumbai. It is the centre of India's film industry, and so has earned the nickname 'Bollywood'. The people of Mumbai love going to the cinema to watch action-packed adventures that are full of traditional singing and dancing.

The Wasa *is a 64-gun Swedish warship that sank in Stockholm harbour on its first voyage in 1628. It was raised from the seabed in 1961, restored, and put on display in its own special museum.*

▶

▼ *Many office workers live in the outskirts of Mumbai and travel into Victoria Station, in the centre of the city, every day on overcrowded trains.*

People of the North

 These restored turf-covered houses show how the Vikings lived in Newfoundland. Today, more than half a million people live on the island.

The world's northern islands are cold places to live, and those above the **Arctic Circle** are often surrounded by ice. Many of the islands of the North Atlantic and Arctic Oceans were first explored by Viking sailors in the ninth century. These sailors often followed the flight of birds, sometimes releasing a raven from their boat and then sailing in the same direction. In this way they sailed to the Shetlands, the Faroes and Iceland. Then, a Viking named Eric the Red sailed his **longship** from Iceland to Greenland. Around 1002, his son, known as Leif the Lucky, travelled even further. He named the first land he and his sailors reached *Helluland*, meaning 'Land of Flat Stones'. This was probably Baffin Island, in present-day Canada. He then sailed south to Newfoundland.

World's largest island

Greenland is the largest island in the world, yet it belongs to a much smaller country – Denmark. The first people to settle there were Inuit hunters, who crossed the ice sheet from the mainland of North America. The island was named by Eric the Red, who found summer grass growing near the shore and gave the island a name that would attract more settlers from Iceland. Today, the islanders still live near the coast, because most of the island is covered by an **ice cap** that is more than 3 kilometres thick in places. Near the south coast,

These steep-roofed houses are in Nuuk, the capital of Greenland. The town has a population of nearly 14,000.

Greenlanders (most of whom are a mixture of Inuit and Scandinavians) manage to graze sheep and grow potatoes and cabbages.

The Land of Flat Stones

Today, about 10,000 people call Baffin Island home. Almost half of them live in the town of Iqaluit (which means 'place of fish' in the Inuit language). In 1999, the island became part of the new Canadian territory of Nunavut, which was formed as an Inuit homeland. There are very few hours of daylight during the winter in Iqaluit, and **blizzards** are frequent. The temperature often drops to -45 °C. As a result, people like to celebrate the coming of spring, and each April the inhabitants of Iqaluit hold their own festival. There are traditional Inuit games, singing and dancing, snowmobile and dog-team races, as well as lots of hot food.

Despite the cold and snow, people in northern Canada participate in a variety of outdoor winter activities, including igloo-building contests.

Farming and Fishing

Because the coast and the sea are never very far away, people who live on the world's smaller islands often rely on fishing to provide food and income. The people of the Maldives, for example, have built their lives around fishing. They live on more than 200 small coral islands in the Indian Ocean, and many Maldivians go out to sea in fishing boats every day. On larger islands, farming communities often spring up alongside coastal fishing villages. In Sri Lanka (to the east of the Maldives, in the Indian Ocean), about half of the island's workers are employed in farming. The main products are rice, coconuts and Ceylon tea. In recent years, the number of tourists has increased in both Sri Lanka and the Maldives, bringing income and changing many islanders' way of life.

Western Isles

The Western Isles are a group of about 500 islands off the west coast of Scotland. They are divided into the Inner and Outer Hebrides. For centuries, the Hebrideans have been fishers and farmers, especially on small farms called crofts, where they grow crops such as barley. The people also herd sheep on the **moors** and use the wool to weave a world-famous cloth, called Harris **tweed**, which is used for suits and outfits. The cloth is named after Harris, one of the islands of the Outer Hebrides, which is joined by a narrow strip of land to the larger island of Lewis.

Fishing boats in the Maldives. The Maldivians export much of their catch to Sri Lanka and Japan.

Green pastures in the Outer Hebrides, off the coast of Scotland. In 2003, the 800 islanders of Harris jointly bought their island from its millionaire owner, giving them security for the future.

Sicily

The largest island in the Mediterranean, Sicily has been invaded by many different peoples since ancient times. Greeks, Phoenicians, Romans, Arabs and Normans have all settled on the island, which became part of Italy in 1861. Throughout the rich history of the island, Sicilians have farmed their land and fished in the sea. The area around the island's active volcano, Mount Etna, is popular with farmers because volcanic ash makes the soil there especially **fertile**. They grow oranges, lemons and other fruit on the lower slopes of the volcano.

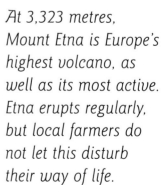

At 3,323 metres, Mount Etna is Europe's highest volcano, as well as its most active. Etna erupts regularly, but local farmers do not let this disturb their way of life.

15

Connecting Islands

Long ago, the only way to travel between islands, as well as from an island to the nearest mainland, was by boat. During the 20th century, however, even the remotest islands, such as Hawaii, which lies in the middle of the Pacific Ocean, became reachable by plane. In recent years, bridges and tunnels have made it easier to travel to islands. The islands of the Florida Keys, at the southern tip of the United States, are connected by a road that travels between the islands on a series of bridges. In Canada, an 11-kilometre bridge connects Prince Edward Island to the mainland. In Denmark, the Storebaelt bridge system, a series of bridges totalling 6,790 metres, crosses a **strait** between the islands of Fyn and Sjaelland.

▲ *The small islands of the Florida Keys are connected by the overseas highway called US Route 1, which is more than 200 kilometres long.*

World's longest suspension bridge

The Akashi Kaikyo Bridge connects Kobe, on Japan's main island of Honshu, with Awaji Island. Another, smaller bridge links Awaji to the much bigger island of Shikoku. With a total

◀

The Akashi Kaikyo Bridge has the tallest towers of any suspension bridge in the world. They measure 283 metres.

length of 3,910 metres and a main span of 1,191 metres, the Akashi Kaikyo is the longest **suspension bridge** in the world. It took 10 years to build and needed to be particularly strong, because this is a region of earthquakes and **typhoons**. In 1995, after seven years of building, there was a major earthquake near Kobe, just over 10 kilometres away from the bridge. Fortunately, there was very little damage to the bridge, which opened on schedule in 1998.

From Honshu to Hokkaido

In 1988, the world's longest rail tunnel opened, linking Japan's two largest islands, Honshu and Hokkaido. This was a huge project, taking 24 years to complete. The tunnel under the Tsugaru Strait is almost 54 kilometres long, and the underwater section is 23 kilometres long. The Channel Tunnel between the island of Great Britain and the European mainland opened six years later. This has a much longer underwater section (38 kilometres).

▶

The port of Hakodate, Japan, is the nearest town to the tunnel entrance on the island of Hokkaido.

Legends and Mysteries

Islands are fascinating places and have given rise to many mysteries. Some of the world's most famous myths and legends have been based on islands, and many popular stories have told of people stranded on desert islands. Famous examples include *Robinson Crusoe*, by Daniel Defoe, *The Swiss Family Robinson*, by Johann Wyss, *Coral Island*, by R. M. Ballantyne, and *Lord of the Flies*, by William Golding. Long before any of these books were written, the Greek philosopher Plato wrote about a brilliant and wealthy island civilization that disappeared beneath the ocean waves. This lost civilization was called Atlantis. Modern historians believe

▲ *A volcanic explosion on the island of Thera created these steep cliffs. But was this the legendary Atlantis?*

that this may have been the Mediterranean island of Thera, which suffered an explosive volcanic eruption around 1500 BC.

Home of the stone giants

Easter Island, in the Pacific Ocean, lies about 3,700 kilometres from the coast of South America. It is most famous for its more than 600 giant stone statues. When Europeans arrived on the island in 1722, some islanders told them that the statues had walked there. For years their

Some of the Easter Island statues have been restored and re-erected. The island has been governed by Chile since 1888.

existence remained a mystery. Who put them up, and why? Historians now believe that the original islanders were Polynesian seafarers, who arrived some time after AD 400. It is thought that they carved the statues from rock and put them up to honour their ancestors. Later, war broke out among the islanders, and many of the statues were knocked down.

The lost colony

In 1587, more than 100 English colonists landed at Roanoke Island, off the coast of what is now North Carolina in the US. A month later, the group's leader, John White, returned to England to get more supplies. Unfortunately, he was delayed there by war with Spain and could not return to Roanoke until 1590. When at last he arrived back on the island, he could find no sign of the colonists, and their houses were in ruins. The only clues were the word 'Croatoan' and the letters 'CRO' carved on two trees. The Croatoans were friendly Native Americans who lived on a nearby island. Soon White was forced to give up his search and return to England. No trace of the 'lost colony' was ever found.

This site on Roanoke Island is a restoration of the lost English colony, the first English settlement in the New World.

19

Tourist Resorts

Islands are very popular with holiday makers because visitors can feel like they are near the sea wherever they are on the island. Small islands in warm seas are especially popular. The Mediterranean Sea has many favourite vacation islands. Mallorca, the largest of the Balearic group of islands, belongs to Spain. During the second half of the 20th century, Mallorca became a very popular destination for **package holidays**. Some resorts grew so quickly that they were soon full of high-rise hotels, shops and restaurants. This has created a great contrast. The resorts are very noisy and busy, while the rest of the island remains quiet and peaceful.

▲ *The lives of villagers in Costa de los Pinos, on the island of Mallorca, carry on in much the same way as they always have, yet they live near a bustling modern tourist resort.*

Land of Wood and Water

The first inhabitants of Jamaica, a large island in the Caribbean Sea, were Native Americans of the Awawak tribe. They called the island *Xaymaca*, meaning 'Land of Wood and Water'. Today, Jamaicans are descended from many other groups: Spaniards brought slaves from Africa in the 16th

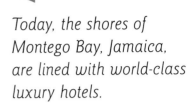

Today, the shores of Montego Bay, Jamaica, are lined with world-class luxury hotels.

century, and then the British invaded and took over the sugar plantations. Jamaica became an independent country in 1962, and since then, people have arrived from China, Syria, and many other parts of the world. Today, many tourists come to the island for all-inclusive luxury holidays at specially developed resorts.

Madeira

In 1419, Portuguese sailors reached an island in the Atlantic Ocean nearly 1,000 kilometres from their mainland port of Lisbon. It was a mountainous, forested island, and they named it *Madeira* (the Portuguese word for 'wood'). Despite later invasions by the Spanish and British, the island still belongs to Portugal. Its pleasant climate, lush green hillsides and beautiful rocky coastline have made it a favourite with holiday makers, who join the 250,000 people who live there all year round. Today, holiday makers can fly from mainland Europe to the international airport on the island in just a few hours.

This traditional building on the northern coast of Madeira is unusual because the **thatched** roof reaches to the ground. They were first built by Portuguese colonists in the 16th century.

Learning about Wildlife

Because islands are surrounded by water and isolated from other lands, their plants and animals are often unique. When explorers and travellers discovered this centuries ago, they realized that the world's islands were perfect places to learn about wildlife. Madagascar, which lies in the Indian Ocean, is a good example. It split away from Africa many millions of years ago, and some of the island's amazing animals – such as **lemurs** and **tenrecs** – exist nowhere else. One of the world's apes, the orangutan, used to live throughout southern China and south-east Asia. Today, it is found only on the islands of Borneo and Sumatra. The orangutan is **endangered** because the forests where it lives are being cut down.

The Enchanted Isles

The Galapagos Islands are a group of 19 islands located 1,000 kilometres west of the mainland of Ecuador. South Americans sailed there in the 16th century, calling the islands the 'Enchanted Isles'. Today, most of the locals are Ecuadorians, living on four of the islands. Some smaller islands are uninhabited. In 1835, the famous British naturalist Charles Darwin arrived in the Galapagos, and he was fascinated to find so

▼ *The ring-tailed lemurs of Madagascar look like monkeys. They live in troops (groups) of up to 40 animals.*

Tourists take a break from their cruise to explore the wonders of the Galapagos Islands.

many unique creatures, including giant tortoises, flightless cormorants and marine iguanas. Today, scientists and interested tourists visit the islands to see the unique wildlife.

Skomer

Skomer is a small, rocky island off the coast of western Wales. Evidence of an Iron Age settlement that may have held up to 200 people has been found on it, and there was a single farm on the island until 1950. Since then, the only people to stay overnight on Skomer are the wildlife warden and people studying the island's amazing variety of bird life. Skomer is now protected as a **nature reserve**. It has about 165,000 breeding pairs of Manx shearwaters (possibly half the world population of this bird), as well as puffins, guillemots, razorbills and kittiwakes.

The nature reserve of Skomer. If people were allowed to live on the Welsh island, the bird colonies would soon be disturbed.

Man-made Islands

Throughout history, people have reclaimed land from the sea, lakes and rivers to make places to live. The original capital of the Aztecs, Tenochtitlan, was built on an island in the middle of Lake Texcoco. The Aztecs then made farming land by creating 'floating gardens' and making their island bigger. After the Aztecs had been conquered by Spanish invaders, the lake was completely drained and is now covered by Mexico City. Across the world, in ancient Egypt, an island in the Nile River, caled Philae, was dedicated to the goddess Isis, and a temple was built in her honour on the island. But when the Aswan High Dam was built, the waters rose, and the island began to disappear. The solution was

▲ *The Temple of Isis, originally built on the ancient Nile island of Philae, can now be visited at its new home on the island of Agilkia.*

to take the temple apart, block by block, and move it to another island, called Agilkia. This island was levelled so that it looked as much as possible like the original ancient island. Today, people visit Agilkia by boat to see the beautiful ancient temple.

Coral islands

Malaita is one of the largest of the Solomon Islands, a country in the South Pacific. The Malaita islanders are skilful sailors and fishermen.

Solomon islanders built these houses on an artificial island in a coral-reef lagoon.

Although Christianity reached the island centuries ago, people there still practise their traditional beliefs, which include worshipping spirits and sharks. In some of the shallow **lagoons**, artificial islands are made from blocks of coral taken from the reef surrounding the lagoon. The Lau lagoon, on the northeast coast of the island, contains more than 60 man-made coral islands.

Island airport

Around 20 million people live in the Kansai region of Japan, near Osaka. When a new airport was needed, the decision was made to build it in Osaka Bay, where aircraft noise would be less disturbing to area residents. This meant building an artificial island more than 4 kilometres long and 2 kilometres wide. First, sand and earth were piled onto the seabed, which was 20 metres beneath the surface. Then, crushed rock was dumped on top from huge floating barges, which were precisely positioned by computers linked to space satellites. The island, which took five years to make, was then connected to the mainland by a road and rail bridge.

Kansai International Airport, in Japan, opened in 1994 and has been a great success.

Faraway Lands

Many of the world's islands are **dependencies** of other countries, and the physical distance between the two locations is often very great. The people of the islands are often descendents of the original colonizers and speak the same language as their **compatriots** on the faraway mainland. The Azores have belonged to Portugal since a Portuguese explorer discovered the nine uninhabited islands in 1431. The islands are 1,300 kilometres west of the Portuguese mainland, in the middle of the Atlantic Ocean. The French island of Réunion, in the Indian Ocean, is more than 9,000 kilometres from the French capital of Paris. It, too, was discovered by a Portuguese sailor, but the French took the island in 1642 and were the first to settle there with African and Indian slaves.

▲ *Market day in Saint-Denis, the capital of Réunion. Most of the island's 700,000 inhabitants are of French, African, Indian or Chinese descent.*

Hawaii

The original inhabitants of the Hawaiian Islands were Polynesians, who sailed there about 2,000 years ago. The islands became the 50th state of the United States in 1959, by which time all the people were US citizens. Today, less than one-fifth of the islanders are of Polynesian ancestry. They have been joined by Europeans, Japanese, Filipinos, Chinese and Koreans. The islands have become a popular tourist destination, especially for Americans, and about seven million visitors arrive every year. Some take 'island-hopping' tours, flying between the four main islands.

The sport of surfing began in Hawaii with the Polynesians. It is still popular today with locals and tourists.

Falklands

The Falkland Islands lie in the South Atlantic. They were first sighted and claimed by an English sailor in 1592, and the islands are still an overseas territory of Britain today – more than 12,500 kilometres from London. Argentina, the nearest country, claims the Falklands (which the Argentineans call *Islas Malvinas*) as its own, and it even fought an unsuccessful war over them in 1982. The islands are covered with rocky moors and **bogs**, and are swept by high winds and heavy rainfall. The islanders are mainly of British descent. They herd sheep and export wool, but their main revenue comes from selling fishing licences to foreign fleets.

More than 90 percent of the work force in the Falkland Islands are engaged in sheep farming or fishing.

27

Pollution and Conservation

Rising sea levels are potentially a great problem for the world's islands. Scientists believe that temperatures around the world are gradually increasing, and that **global warming** could melt some of the ice in the world's two polar regions. This could lead to the submersion of low-lying islands. Tourists are also having a great effect on islands, increasing the amount of litter and other forms of pollution. Yet the people of many small islands have become dependent on tourism. One answer to these problems is to protect islands as national parks. The Mediterranean island of Menorca, for example, has been declared a 'biosphere reserve', and all visitors must pay a small fee to help keep the island clean.

▲ *It's easy to see from this photograph of an island in the Maldives that a rise in sea level would be devastating.*

Logging

In Southeast Asia, many islands were once covered with valuable rainforest. On islands such as Borneo and Sumatra, however, trees have been disappearing at an alarming rate. As mountain forests are cut down for timber, heavy rains wash away the soil and cause the hillsides to become lifeless and barren. At the same time, some of the valuable hardwood trees are being cut down at a much faster rate than they could

Due to aggressive logging, Borneo's rainforest is disappearing even faster than the Brazilian Amazon.

ever grow. These problems affect local islanders as well as wildlife. In some countries, governments are limiting the amount of **logging** in order to conserve the environment.

Nature reserve

Barrow Island, off the northwestern coast of Australia, in the Indian Ocean, has been a nature reserve for a number of years. The island is home to 15 species of land mammals, 7 marine mammal species, 40 reptile species and 110 bird species. But unlike other protected islands, such as Skomer (see page 23), Barrow is also used by industry. Drilling for oil and natural gas began there in the 1950s. Now some researchers are suggesting that the island could be used as a place to bury carbon dioxide – a gas given off in many industrial processes that contributes to global warming. They believe this process is totally safe, but opponents say the gas will leak and cause pollution. Is it worth taking the risk?

Turtle tracks such as these could become increasingly rare if industry continues on Barrow Island.

29

Glossary

ancestors People who lived long ago, from whom people today are descended.

Arctic Circle An imaginary circle around Earth's northern polar region.

blizzards Severe snowstorms, with very strong winds and cold temperatures.

bogs Areas of wet ground; marshes.

boroughs Districts, or sections, of a city.

colonies Areas that are ruled by another country.

compatriots People from the same country.

dependencies Territories that are ruled by another country.

double-hulled With two hulls (main parts of a ship).

endangered At risk of dying out.

equator An imaginary circle around the middle of Earth.

fertile Very rich and capable of producing good crops.

global warming A rise in temperature all over the world.

harpoons Long, pointed pieces of metal or wood used to spear and catch fish.

ice cap A thick, permanent covering of ice.

lagoons Areas of shallow water near the coast, surrounded by coral or sand.

lemurs Animals similar to monkeys.

logging Cutting down trees for timber.

longship A narrow wooden Viking ship with oars and a square sail.

moors Open land with few trees that is often covered with heather.

nation People who live together under a single government; a country.

nature reserve A piece of land or water where animals and plants are protected.

package holidays Holidays arranged by a travel agent that include fares and accommodation for an all-inclusive price.

parliament A group or meeting of people who make a country's laws.

stockades Fences of tall wooden stakes, used for defence.

strait A narrow channel of water.

suspension bridge A bridge that has its roadway suspended from cables.

tenrecs Animals similar to hedgehogs.

terraces Flat, ledge-like pieces of ground on a mountain slope.

thatched With a roof made of straw or rushes.

totem poles Huge posts carved by some Native Americans with figures and animals (called totems) from ancient legends.

tribal groups Groups of people with common ancestry, customs, and beliefs.

tweed A thick, woolen fabric.

typhoons Severe, destructive tropical storms; also called 'hurricanes'.

Index